Undisturbed

A Brief History of the Sheffield General Cemetery

Written by Jane Horton

for

The Friends of the General Cemetery

Published by The Friends of the General Cemetery

Written by Jane Horton supported by Adrian Hallam and Joan Sewell, Ark Design Management Ltd, and researched by Tanya Schmoller, Alan and Sylvia Jackson, Jane Horton, Adrian Hallam, Joan Sewell, Lucy Sacker, Julia Duggleby and James Buck.

Layout Design by Andrew Pettigrew

Edited by Tanya Schmoller

Printed by Unicorn Press

ISBN 0-9539994-0-8
Copyright Friends of the General Cemetery 2001
Revised edition 2002

Acknowledgements
The Friends of the General Cemetery gratefully acknowledge Sheffield City Council Leisure Services and Stephen McClarence for the use of numerous images in this publication.

Illustrations
Sheffield City Council Leisure Services: pp. 7, 9(x2), 11, 17, 23, 24, 25, 63.
Ark Design Management Ltd: pp. 10, 12, 16.
Stephen McClarence: pp. 51, 59
All other images are in FOGC s Collection.

Contents

Preface

Sheffield's General Cemetery is one of the city's finest historic assets. It contains nine listed buildings and monuments, three at Grade II*. It has an important place in the history of cemetery design both nationally and internationally, because of its unusual lay out and Egyptianate style, as one of the country's earliest cemeteries and because it is likely that it influenced John Claudius Loudon's seminal book On the Laying out of Cemeteries, which was to be fundamental to development of cemeteries in this country. The site also has a significant place in the history of parks in Britain, as it utilised the skills of one of the great park designers of the 19th century, Robert Marnock. A designated Conservation area, in 1999 it was added to the National Register of Historic Parks and Gardens as a Grade II site, one of only six places in South Yorkshire to attain this status.

The cemetery's founders struggled to make a profit on the cemetery in the early years, but then must have been surprised at how busy it became (A total of 87,000 people are buried there). However, if they visited the site today, they would be shocked. The General Cemetery became sadly neglected when the Cemetery Company abandoned it in the 1950s. Today some visitors comment on its tumbledown state, but many more appreciate its beauty, and realise what a quiet treasure trove it is. The Friends of the General Cemetery work to save the site from neglect, and have commenced the first phase of its restoration with the Gatehouse project. It is used by schools, students and community groups to extend their understanding of Victorian history, geology, religion, art, change, health, politics and economics.

The cemetery's history can be understood through examination of the Cemetery Company's minutes and those of its occupants through burial records, census returns, obituaries and newspapers articles. This first history of the cemetery has been put together to meet an increasing demand for information about the site, and serves only as an introduction. For the enthusiast, there is much more to find out, through looking at the inscriptions on the gravestones and examining archive material.

Background

The burial of the dead was revolutionised in the first half of the 19th century. People were fast moving from the countryside to the town, where there was much disease, and death rates soared. Sheffield was one of the fastest growing towns in England. Industry created unbearable living conditions and the foul emissions from factories combined with Sheffield's hilly environment to produce dreadful air pollution adding to the poverty, squalor and lack of space.

Population

The population of England doubled during the first half of the nineteenth century, from nine million in 1801 to eighteen million by 1851. England also became predominantly urban with 54% of the population living in towns in 1851, compared to 20% in 1801. Growth was concentrated in urban areas particularly in the Northern and Midland industrial centres of Manchester, Leeds and Birmingham. In Sheffield there was dramatic population growth, trebling from 45,758 in 1801 to 135,310 by 1851.

As Sheffield grew, so did the problem of where to bury the dead. Churchyards were full to bursting - health hazards in themselves; body snatching was a constant threat. Most significant of all, the growing reaction of the non conformist movement against the monopoly of the Established Church acted as a real catalyst for change. (The Established Church could either deny burial to non conformists or insist on their going through rites from which such groups were consciously dissenting.)

Illustration by Phiz for
Bleak House by Charles Dickens

3

Dickens on Dead Citizens

Dickens in The Uncommercial Traveller wrote: *'The rot and mildew and dead citizens was the main smell in London's churches, where the decay of dead citizens in the vaults below produces a strong kind of invisible snuff so that when we stamp our feet to warm them … dead citizens arise in heavy clouds.'*

Body Snatching

The extent of body snatching at the beginning of the 19th century was a real cause of concern and prompted the introduction of the Anatomy Act in 1832, which helped control this gruesome trade. (Bodies were stolen to supply corpses for dissections). Boundary walls in the new cemeteries of the 19th century reflected a need for security in contrast to the open and vulnerable nature of churchyards where body snatching was easy. At the General Cemetery the minutes of the Company show that security guards were employed, and the high wall around the cemetery supports the need for protection from body snatchers.

In 1834, a group of non conformists formed the General Cemetery Company, in the district of Sharrow in Sheffield, to address these problems … and make money.

Cemeteries had already been established abroad, often in regions colonised by the English.

For example, as early as 1767 a cemetery was founded in Calcutta, marking a key stage in the city's development and establishing Calcutta as the centre for British power in India.

The greatest influence on English cemetery design was to come from France where problems of overcrowding and the disgusting nature of churchyards had already prompted drastic measures. In 1784 the main burial ground of central Paris was closed and in the following two years all bones and remains were cleared and placed in catacombs. Cemeteries were then established in three parts of the city, the largest of the three called Cimitiere Pere Lachaise. The first burial took place there in 1804. This cemetery had aspects that were to influence developments in England (and specifically Sheffield) in terms of layout and economics.

It was not until 1820 that the first cemetery company was formed in England. The first significant private cemetery was established in London at Kensal Green in 1832. From then until the establishment of local burial boards in 1852, cemeteries were created in many cities, each one unique and often a reflection of the local cultural and social influences.

The rise of non conformists in Sheffield is clearly displayed in the General Cemetery. Class boundaries were changed for ever by the establishment of this new group of people whose wealth was not based on land ownership, but through their significant role in forming the new industrial base of Sheffield. Their success is exemplified in the figure of Sheffield's greatest steel baron, Mark Firth, who is buried in the General Cemetery.

Non Conformism

Industrialisation had provided new niches of opportunity, leading to new professions -surveyors, architects, shopkeepers, bankers, engineers and designers. These people earned more money than labourers and had different social values. This class also identified with the strong dissenting tradition in Sheffield s religion and politics which allowed them to assert their independence from the gentry who were more likely to be Anglican and conservative. The term non conformism describes this group of people, also sometimes referred to as dissenters.

Whatever the commercial desires, and religious and political posturing of the subscribers of the Sheffield General Cemetery Company, there was also a philanthropic basis to their actions. The negative publicity over the poor state of the towns burials and the dangers to the health of Sheffield citizens ensured that something happened. Several epidemics had swept the town in the early 1830s, and burial space by the mid 1830s was at crisis point.

Inadequate Provision for the Dead

A newspaper article from The Sheffield Independent of March 1834 stated that: The very inadequate Provision which is made in Sheffield for the burial of the Dead, has for a long time engaged the public attention. The article goes on to explain that: The general features of the country immediately surrounding the Town of Sheffield, are in a remarkable degree favourable to the establishment of a ...place of interment.

Smith s Report into the Health of Towns

Smith s graphic report on Sheffield of 1845, although post-dating the initiation of the General Cemetery, explains one major reason for the establishment of it:

'Complaints are made of the offensive nature of the interments within the town. One churchyard in the middle of the town is peculiarly offensive. It is very much crowded with bodies and as the soil is considerably above the level of the surrounding street, the exudation of putrid liquid from the soil is visible to the eye and offensive to the smell. The soil, being of a tenacious clay, the decay of the bodies is slow; where the graves are opened the skeletons are often found still articulated and their exhumation is most offensive to the inhabitants residing within sight of the burial ground. A cemetery has just been established at some distance by a Joint Stock Company, under good regulations. It is beginning to be resorted to and it is hoped that the bulk of the interments will hereafter be made in this or some other similar place; for whether we consider the health and comfort of the inhabitants, or the softer feelings of the relatives of the dead, or generally feelings of public decency we must approve of the arrangement of having burial places in a remote and undisturbed locality.'

The Early Years

The concept of commercial burial was relatively new when the General Cemetery was first established. In 1834, at the first meeting of subscribers, 24 of Sheffield's great and good gathered at the Cutlers Hall to consider the prospect of a new burial ground, at some distance in the countryside (Cemetery Company Minutes).

THOMAS ASLINE WARD.

Nearly every one of the subscribers at this first meeting was a member of this newly defined middle class: with merchants, manufacturers, doctors, surgeons, and bankers among them. Four of the original subscribers were at some point Master Cutlers of Sheffield, and one a Mayor. Thomas Asline Ward, Master Cutler, diarist, and founder of the Literary and Philosophical Society was the most notable of the group, and the prime mover of the General Cemetery development.

The nine acres of land upon which the General Cemetery was built were purchased from Henry Wilson of Westbrook, a snuff manufacturer, for £1,900. He owned a snuff mill a few hundred yards further along the Porter valley. Only five acres of the land purchased were to be enclosed at first as it was considered to be sufficient for several generations. This was a very eligible piece of land, meeting all the market requirements, conveniently close to where the new prosperous dissenting classes were establishing their homes in the new clean suburbs of the west of Sheffield, principally Nether Edge. It was, in real terms, a relatively cheap piece of land, being on a northerly slope and hence less attractive for residential development. The valley provided a good opportunity for the cemetery designer to meet the demanding requirements of the shareholders. Henry Wilson was concerned to ensure that the design of the cemetery would not detract from the beauty of the Porter Valley, because the snuff mill was situated in an idyllic spot. Two drafts of a conveyance document were produced, detailing the proposals for the site. These conveyance documents allowed for the transfer of four fields in this rural area to the Cemetery Company, and the diversion of the River Porter to make a cleaner line at the base of the site.

Samuel Worth, architect, won a competition to design the cemetery. The project he was to undertake was described by the company shareholders as an undertaking of no ordinary magnitude (Cemetery Company Minutes).

Samuel Worth wins a competition

A competition for a scheme for the site was launched and won by Samuel Worth. The Sheffield Independent of 1st August 1834 advertised from Samuel Worth s office for tenders for work on the new cemetery for the erection of a bridge and walling; also for sundry excavations required for a proposed diversion of the course of the Porter Brook, and the forming of a Carriage Entrance Road to the intended Cemetery.

Worth's plans for the site were ambitious and took full advantage of the steeply sloping site. The cemetery layout gave Worth a great opportunity to demonstrate his architectural and landscape design skills. In this first phase of the cemetery's life, Robert Marnock, the garden design and botanic expert, acted as a consultant to the works.

The New Cemetery

By 1836 The Sheffield Mercury reported the opening of:
'the new cemetery, a pleasant grassy lawn by the side of the River Porter, thickly shadowed over by Oak, Ash and Elder.'
And in the same year The Sheffield Independent referred to: *'the crowds of people who are in the habit of visiting this very attractive and interesting place. Whites directory report of 1837 stated that the cemetery is indisputably one of the most beautiful establishments of its kind in the kingdom, and though some of its chief attractions are attributable to the situation, it is much indebted to the skill and taste of the architect, Mr S Worth, who has made it a delightful spot for the perambulations of the living, and a safe depository for the dead.'*

The design theme of the plan that was accepted by the Cemetery Company was eclectic in style, and reflected Worth's desire to harness the already developing classical vision of the landscape in the Porter Valley. With obelisks at the Cemetery Avenue (at the junction with Manchester Turnpike Road, now Ecclesall Road) entrance the

approach was lined by lime trees leading to the Gate House over the river Porter. The road was flanked by a low wall on either side.

The approach was an integral part of the landscape plan. In fact an earlier Worth plan for this entrance avenue is much more dramatic than the design that was eventually executed. It allowed for a gently winding pathway, starting at ground level, but building up gradually, so that at the point it reaches and crosses the Porter, the path is raised 12 feet in the air, with parapets on either side. Whatever the reason for this plan being abandoned, the fact that it was drawn up at all demonstrates how grand the vision Samuel Worth had for the site, which apart from this most flamboyant part of the proposal, was executed according to plan.

The gatehouse (Grade II*) was important in setting the first impression of the cemetery and would have been clearly visible rising in tiers up the hillside beyond. The main gateway, side lodges and supporting bridge were designed in a classical revival style and made of sandstone.

The building sat upon a substantial wide bridge that spanned the Porter Brook (possibly making classical reference to crossing to the afterlife over the River Styx).

The Gatehouse Gates

There used to be elaborate wrought iron gates for the gatehouse which survived into the 1970s. However, these were not the original gates: they belong to the later Victorian period. The Cemetery Company minutes of November 1836 refer to a quotation for wooden gates for this entrance, but no evidence of these survives.

The original landscape plan for the cemetery made much use of the dramatic hillside setting. The potential of this steeply sloping site was obvious to the shareholders who discussed its merits in their first meeting at the Cutlers Hall in Sheffield: The land affords an opportunity for executing a plan which though novel will be of singular advantage to the company (Cemetery Company Minutes).

The hillside was quarried to provide the stone for the buildings. This increased the depth of views across the complete landscape. The main path through the site sweeps up the hill in a giant back-to-front 'S' shape.

Promotional painting of the Cemetery by Hofland, 1837

The serpentine sweep through the cemetery is emphasised by the two curving tiers of catacombs close to the gatehouse entrance of the site that follow the line of the main path up the hill.

The catacomb doorways were designed to have iron gates at the entrances once they became occupied. Some of these were ordered but only a few catacombs were ever used and there is no proof that they were installed. Below the catacombs, close to the point at which the steps from the catacombs descend to the Porter's edge, a footbridge was established.

The Catacombs

The catacombs proved unpopular. Only ten of these were sold in the first 10 years. By far the majority of burials that took place were of skilled artisans, not the wealthy dissenters the Company was hoping for. This may have been a surprise to the Company Directors, who were no doubt aware of the successes at Pere Lachaise in Paris. The lack of popularity of catacombs as a burial method may have been partly due to price, but it was certainly cheaper than erecting a monument over a vault which many chose to do. A more likely reason is that Sheffield people had a reluctance to adopt this fashion in such a serious matter as burial. The expression of individualism, so central to the beliefs of the new dissenters class, is satisfied more readily by the array of varied monumental styles that is the dominant theme across the cemetery. That was something catacombs failed to offer: they were a relatively anonymous form of burial. They had been expensive to create, helped to unify a stunning landscape, but were not profitable.

The main pathway from the turnpike road was cobbled, traces of which can still be seen beneath the tarmac along the road today. (The Cemetery Company minutes refer to the last layer of stone being laid on this road in October 1835.) As the path curves up the hill, views across the valley were planned. The main path sweeps back to the west half way up the hill, and draws the eye to the chapel, which sits squarely in the middle of the site. This building, also designed by Worth, is the centrepiece of the original cemetery plan. The chapel was designed in a direct line of sight to the portico of the Wesley School (now King Edward's, a similar classical building built in the same year as the chapel). Also visible are the glasshouses of the Botanical Gardens, again built in the same year as the chapel, adding to views in what was becoming a classical landscape in the Porter valley.

The Botanical Gardens

The Sheffield Botanical and Horticultural Society, formed in June 1833 with the intention of creating a botanical garden to promote healthy recreation and self improvement. Robert Marnock won a competition for the design and layout of the gardens and became its first curator. The garden was created on 18 acres of south facing farmland on the northern slopes of the Porter valley. Admission to Sheffield Botanical Gardens, opened in 1836, was limited to shareholders and annual subscribers only with the exception of four Gala days per year when the gates opened to the general public.

The chapel (Grade II*) is made of sandstone in the classical style. The front of the chapel has a Greek Doric portico with substantial columns beneath. Under the portico, there is a large Egyptian-style doorway. Above the door there is a sculpted relief panel of a dove. Each elevation had four simply framed Egyptian windows, each with hexagonal iron fretwork.

Painting the Chapel

It would appear that there was an intention to paint the inside of the chapel, although the architect was informed that the committee would not pay any further expense of colouring.

Robert Marnock

Robert Marnock designed the Botanical Gardens in Sheffield, became its curator, went on to design the second phase of the cemetery in 1850, and then the Botanic Gardens in Regents Park, London, in 1840, and also worked with the famous park and garden designer Paxton. He was asked to inspect the laying out and planting of the original cemetery and a donation was made to him in 1837 in acknowledgement of this service. In later life, following a successful career nationally, Marnock returned to Sheffield where he carried out work on some large private estates and gardens. He saw the cemetery he designed taken over by rows of gravestones, so perhaps not surprising that he favoured cremation and was himself cremated.

A Cold Building

Although the chapel was principally designed for funerals, soon after it was built Sunday services were held in the building. Evening services, however, were soon discontinued due to the severe coldness of the place (Cemetery Company Minutes).

The area behind the chapel was deeply quarried as the cemetery was being built, and the plan, partially carried out, was to build up vaults in this area, so that the area would not have to be filled in. This would then provide a large quantity of graves, of much greater depth than normal. This provided the General Cemetery with the deepest single grave plot in the country, finally accommodating 96 bodies. Stone from this area was used to build the main cemetery structures.

Towards the west the steep quarry edge was planned to be left as rough walls with edges cut (Cemetery Company Minutes).

This is the steep walled edge on the west of the cemetery that has now been concreted, and on top of which today sits a towering set of offices, erected in around 1990.

The main path in front of the chapel curves up to the west towards the cemetery office. (Grade II) and the southerly entrance of the site. Again heavily influenced by the Egyptian style, the square building has pairs of long sloping simply framed windows on each side. The building was originally in an elegant setting with a weeping silver beech to its East, a formal garden to the north and two symmetrically aligned pathways to the south, designed to lead to two equally placed Egyptian gateways opening on to the bridleway near Sharrow Head. It is not clear whether both were eventually built but one was completed in

May 1836 (Grade II*). The gateways were designed in Egyptian style, with iron rail gates, richly ornamented with symbolic references: snakes eating their tails: a symbol of mortality, and facias, symbols of unity. Above each gate was a winged orb, a symbol of Egyptian mythology.

The General Cemetery Company offices

From the date of the first burial in the General Cemetery in May 1836 the General Cemetery Company had mixed fortunes. Its starting point had been ambitious, and it is clear that the Company struggled as a result of the excessive cost of achieving its vision for the site.

The original landscape layout had an air of confidence about it, as the Directors' words, as well as the amount of money spent on the development, demonstrate. Only the year before they had stated that the whole undertaking has acquired a magnitude and incurred difficulties which far surpass what was first contemplated. (Directors' report).

Hofland s engraving of the General Cemetery

Egyptian Influences

The General Cemetery clearly derived a stylistic influence of the Egyptian from the Pere Lachaise in Paris and was the first cemetery in Britain to do so. Indeed the influence of the Egyptian is strong and consistent throughout the cemetery landscape design, and then echoed in the styling of many of the monuments. This is striking and unusual because the Egyptian Revival was mostly used in Britain only as elements and lines in design.

The annual meetings of Directors for the first few years often took place in the Cutlers Hall, an indication of the status of the Cemetery Company in Sheffield society. However, the whole amount expended was around £13,000, a very significant sum in the 1830s. To promote the Cemetery, the Company commissioned Hofland, a local painter, to produce an elaborate painting and engravings. These are the only early surviving images of the cemetery that are known of.

The 1838 Directors' Report comments on the unparalleled depression in the state of trade and commerce that Sheffield, in common with other parts of the country, were suffering. The fees set by the Company must have been too high as the early table of charges were substantially reduced. The shareholders were not going to get as good an immediate return on their investment as they probably expected. This, combined with the need to pay for the investment of erecting a mason's workshop, meant the cemetery company was not able to report a good dividend.

Picturesque and Enchanting

Situated beyond the precinct of the town; in its scenery, picturesque and enchanting, exhibiting amidst the stillness which befits the repose of the dead, so many forms of life to remind the spectator rather of the future resurrection than of the temporary dissolution of the body. (General Cemetery Directors report 1837)

The First Occupant of the Cemetery

This was Mary Ann Fish who died of consumption at the age of 24. From there it took six years to sell the first 1,000 burials and it was not until the opening of the Anglican Cemetery that the Company really became profitable. The early years were dogged by theft, vandalism, problems with stone masons, policies favouring Anglican burials, and relatively poor sales.

Pauper Burials

For every pauper buried the Cemetery Company gained five shillings. The General Cemetery had a distinct advantage when it came to multiple interments. Many graves had been pre-dug and built up in many parts of the site, allowing numerous burials. In fact the General Cemetery seems to have had more pauper burials in a single grave plot than anywhere else in the country. Many pauper graves list burial numbers in the 70s and 80s; with several in the 90s. The highest number in a single plot recorded in Sheffield General Cemetery is 96.

John Claudius Loudon

It was JC Loudon, well known as champion of the parks movement in 19th century England, who became hugely influential with his strong views regarding the nature and laying out of cemeteries. The publication of his book On the Laying Out of Cemeteries in 1843, represented a landmark for the cemetery movement In it Loudon dealt with every aspect of cemetery design. He expressed strong views on the style that should be employed in cemeteries and emphasized that they could offer instruction by example in many fields of study, including sculpture and botany. Loudon promoted the use of hardy trees and shrubs in cemeteries, many recently introduced from abroad, and suggested that cemeteries could be made into arboreta or botanical gardens. Loudon had significant connections with Sheffield that may have influenced some of the information given in his book. The influence on J.C. Loudon can be seen in his book On the Laying out of Cemeteries published in 1843. He and his wife had visited the General Cemetery in May 1839. His book proposes a plan for the laying out of a cemetery on a hilly site. While it does not acknowledge the General Cemetery as its source, it can be no coincidence that the plan is almost a replica of the General Cemetery layout, which he had visited only a few years previously. In fact Loudon then went on to execute this design at Southampton Cemetery in 1843.

However, in this period the number of pauper burials saved the business. Cemetery companies contracted with Poor Law authorities for their burial at a per pauper rate. By the 1840s the wealthy, for the most part, were still not choosing the General Cemetery as their final resting place. Even the revenue from pauper burials, which the Company relied on, was under threat. By 1841 the company was tabling its concerns about the prevailing prejudice of the cemetery in not having been consecrated in the form of the Established Church (Cemetery Company Minutes).

The Directors' Report is more specific: the cemetery has not hitherto had anything like a reasonable share of pauper funerals, a partiality which it is hoped a proper representation to the Board of Guardians (of the Poor) will do something to prevent·

Interim remedies such as payment of an admission fee to the cemetery were introduced, but still in 1845 the Directors minuted the recent legislation allowing pauper interments only in consecrated ground. They pondered further why the resting place was not more popular when its picturesque and architectural attractions were so great and concluded that objections exist, which operate disadvantageously, and which are not confined to the operative classes, but also to the wealthy and opulent. (In fact the General Cemetery contains a pauper's grave, a single grave plot, with 96 interments, probably the most populated single plot in the country.)

In this first period of the cemetery's history the monument designs were overwhelmingly classical. It was not until the mid-19th century, when ground was consecrated, that the cross motif and pointed headstone began to appear. The classical headstones and larger-scale monuments of this period are largely Greek Revival style, with classical symbolism including the use of classical patterning, simple curved top gravestones and overt symbols such as urns, pyramids and columns. There are a significant number of obelisks from this early period, echoing the overall styling of the cemetery. The majority of the monuments from this period are of Brincliffe Blue sandstone, quarried locally. Luckily, this stone resists weathering and retains much of its detailing.

Stone Masonry in the Cemetery

The Cemetery Company soon realised that money was to be made in stone masonry, and within a year had employed a skilful and ingenious mason. This mason was charged with securing the richest display of elegance, propriety and taste in the varied memorials which affection may place upon the ashes of departed friends.

In 1838 a stone mason s workshop was established on the site. Judging from the number of stones in the cemetery that bear the Cemetery Company s mark, it would appear that the company stone mason was a popular choice when gravestones were commissioned. By 1845 the mason s skills were being fulsomely praised in the company reports: his talents have been deservedly appreciated and hitherto secured the richest display of elegance, propriety and taste in the varied memorials that now adorn this city of the dead.

However, other stone masons were at work in the neighbourhood in the early years: notably Edwin Smith (father of Theophilus), and Joseph Hadfield, but also Benjamin Fidler and the Eatons of Cemetery Road. Various Company Minutes betray a financial penalty if the Cemetery Company s mason was not used, and indeed the right to reject stones produced by other masons. It appears, on further reading, that the financial penalty the Company would have liked to impose on other masons work entering the cemetery was never applied: there are resolutions recorded in the minutes not to act on this ruling.

Theophilus Smith

Theophilus made a name for himself as an early documentary photographer, but he was also an excellent draughtsman and monumental sculptor. He had a genuine interest in the principles of Christian monument design and published several catalogues on the subject. In fact Theophilus is regarded as one of the three most important monument designers at work in the period, with particular reference to his wrought-iron metalwork. The General Cemetery has many examples of his work, though much of his work was destroyed in 1978.

Theophilus Smith had his finger on the pulse of the monument market. Firstly the development of monument templates reflected the growing commercialisation of the burial market, and indeed an understanding of the new concept of commercialism, which asserted itself formally in the Great Exhibition of 1851. He also developed the sense of private property in his elaborate and emphatic use of wrought-iron railing around monuments.

Sadly, Theophilus s personal and working life became a disaster following a carriage accident that crippled him. He became unable to work, had no money and became an alcoholic. He was charged with wife beating and died in disgrace.

By the end of the 1840s the cemetery landscape was by no means overflowing with gravestones. Although sections were beginning to fill up, grassy slopes were still much in evidence. In this period the majority of the grander monuments were boldly neoclassical in style. It was not until 1849 that Edwin Smith established his Marble and Stone Works on Cemetery Road, out of which would come some of the cemetery's best designed and executed monuments.

The Dissenters Wall

The Cemetery Company made plans. Towards the mid 1840s there was a flurry of activity, leading to the establishment of a new area of consecrated ground in 1850 to overcome the reluctance of the established church to use the cemetery. A low wall, from the top to the bottom of the site, the perimeter wall of the original cemetery, now became the division between the non conformist and the Anglican burial ground. It became a symbol of the division and known as the Dissenters' wall. Another key factor in the Cemetery Company's decision to expand the cemetery was a change in the law that stated that all pauper burials should take place in consecrated ground. This major blow meant that the General Cemetery was excluded from burying paupers in the non conformist ground.

The General Cemetery commissioned Robert Marnock, who by now had a well established reputation, and William Flockton, who was by 1846 a well regarded architect, and son of a builder, to develop a new Anglican cemetery alongside the original site. Flockton and Marnock had already worked together on the development of George Wostenholm's house in Nether Edge, and Wostenholm was, in 1846, on the General Cemetery Company's committee.

Younger than Samuel Worth, Flockton's design for the Anglican Chapel (Grade II) was more concerned with detail and is a confident

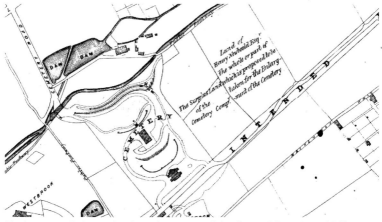

Flockton s preliminary plan for enlargement of the General Cemetery, 1846

Neo-Gothic work that contrasts totally with the neoclassical non conformist chapel. The juxtaposition of these two opposing building styles is something that makes this cemetery unique. The spire of the Anglican chapel would have been very prominent from anywhere in the city and in proportion to the rest of the building is disproportionately large. Flockton played up its size to give it prominence in the landscape.

Architect s impression for the design of the new Anglican Chapel

Whites Directory entry for 1849 also states that the New Cemetery Road has just opened.

The Developing Anglican Cemetery

The Builder in September 1849 describes the developing Anglican cemetery: *The New cemetery for the establishment, now in course of formation beside the original cemetery at Sheffield, approaches towards completion. The improvements comprise a new carriage road, 45 feet wide, passing the cemetery and in connection with which a bridge has been erected over the River Porter. The church, with its tall spire, is nearly finished.*

Whites Directory Entry

Whites Directory entry for 1849 refers to: *'the new handsome church in the decorated style of architecture, with a lofty spire and tower.'* and makes reference to the beauty of the valley: *'the chapel and the church, standing near the crown of the acclivity, form conspicuous objects in the beautiful vale of the Porter, on the opposite side of which are the Botanical gardens and many handsome villas.'*

Marnock submitted a plan for the planting of the consecrated ground in 1850, and the planting and supply of shrubs was tendered for. Mr Law, the curator of the Botanical Gardens who succeeded Robert Marnock in that role, was this time asked to give his opinion on the planting of the grounds. By August 1850, the planting could be seen to full advantage. The company report says: the beauty of its scenery, when taken in connection with the adjacent Botanical Gardens, may be considered unrivalled in this or any other country.

Marnock s plan of 1851 for the Anglican part of the General Cemetery

Despite the fact that the development costs for this new phase again exceeded calculations, at £25,000, the company acknowledged that what was achieved for that price was quite exceptional. Flockton was not paid immediately for all his work, in view of the still difficult situation of the Cemetery Company.

Trade picked up quickly however, and the period from 1850 through to 1890 was a very busy one. 1849 ended with the 'terrible visitation of cholera' which meant that trade got off to a prosperous start in 1850. From 1852 through to 1857 there was a sequence of Burial Acts that helped to regulate cemeteries and effectively endorsed the innovation of the joint stock companies, such as the General Cemetery.

The Sheffield Parish Burial Board

> The Sheffield Parish Burial Board was established following the 1852 Act. The first Burial Board cemeteries in Sheffield to be set up were at Darnall and Attercliffe. Both of these were relatively small, restrained in design and geographically remote from the General Cemetery. In any case they did not represent any competition to the class of person at which the General Cemetery was aimed. It was in this period that the landscape design of the Anglican Cemetery was altered, from the romantic curved lines designed by Marnock, in line with the style of the Burial Board Cemeteries, to make it more utilitarian, and certainly to make more space.

In 1857 Wardsend Cemetery was established. This catered for a wealthier class than the two earlier Burial Board cemeteries established in Sheffield and may have taken some trade away from the General Cemetery. In 1860 Burngreave cemetery was established and added real competition to the General Cemetery. It had two chapels by Flockton, and was substantial (27 acres). However, the population of Sheffield was by now so big (185,155) that there was plenty of trade to go round. A local churchyard was the nearest threat to business. The well established Anglican burial ground at Ecclesall attracted many well-to-do people.

Sandford s Walk

> In 1853 the Anglican chaplain of the consecrated chapel, George Sandford, asked for the privilege of planting beeches and limes in the walk intersecting the consecrated ground. This avenue then became known as Sandford s Walk and these trees have grown to a majestic size today.

The Sheffield Flood

In 1864 the minutes note the dreadful calamity of the Sheffield flood. Sixty plus bodies were brought for burial (in fact a total of seventy seven flood victims are buried in the cemetery) and later the body of John Gunson was buried in the General Cemetery. He was the resident deputy engineer blamed for the dam burst that caused the flood, but later exonerated from blame. This well documented national tragedy is a story well encapsulated in the burials in the General Cemetery, thanks to another cemetery resident, Samuel Harrison, who wrote the first account of the flood.

From 1863 into the early 1870s there were a few mishaps. Heavy rains led to the river Porter breaking its banks on several occasions. The walls had to be rebuilt more than once and a new river wall was erected in 1871. This was accompanied by the repair of the walk beside the River Porter in the section that runs past the cemetery. This was dedicated in 1871 and designated a public road. The problem of flooding at the base of the cemetery was also to cost the Company significant sums in the future.

The Disagreeable Management at the Cemetery

In 1865 The Sheffield Daily Telegraph reported disagreeable mismanagement at the General Cemetery. This referred to a growing battle over vicars fees, which escalated in 1867 to become a court case. The vicars case rested on the fact that where there were no burial spaces left in graveyards in their parishes, or no graveyards at all, they were still entitled to a fee per body from their district. Of the seven chapels up for debate, three had chapel yards and four did not. This dispute simply reinforces the economic basis of burial in this era and in this instance the Company s profit margin was under threat.

Between 1870 and 1900 the cemetery was extremely busy. The minutes show, for the most part, transactions for stone and submissions for monuments. One was rejected as inappropriate: a proposed flat marble tablet covered with a glass dome. (Later it was agreed that a medallion could be inserted instead.) In 1876 water was supplied to the lodges at the gate house, following complaints about offensive matter being allowed to flow into the Porter from this point.

However, because the Company was so busy, it appears that it overlooked the fact that the grounds were not being looked after properly. By 1898 the minutes record complaints being received about the state of the grounds, and a five-page report was submitted on the state of the Company.

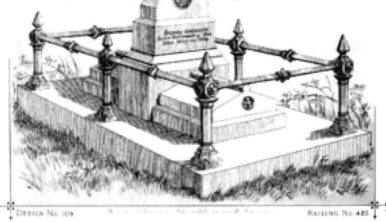

Monuments of this period of the cemetery's history were more varied than in the earlier period. Though still predominantly of local sandstone, the advent of the railway in the 1840s meant it was easier and cheaper to bring stone from other areas, so Italian Marble began to be imported, also Aberdeen Granite, and Larvikite from Norway. In this period, with increasing demand for gravestones, coupled with increasingly mechanised production processes, it became possible to develop gravestone templates, machine carved, which people could tailor to their wishes. Pattern books began to appear, and designer Theophilus Smith was swift to employ this method as a way of illustrating the many designs on offer. This trend

Template design for memorial with railings by Theophilus Smith

signalled a gradual but definite decline in the standard of gravestone design. From now on there would be less hand-carving and greater uniformity of gravestones.

The War Period

From the turn of the century onwards, the Company minutes document many repairs to the grounds. In 1909, gates were repaired. In 1912 the lodges, chapel and the offices were re-slated. The trees were pruned in 1913 and dead ones removed. Sandford's walk was straightened with a flagged stone path added.

In 1913, the path between the office and the chapel was turfed over and the Dissenters' wall built up. This created more plots, an indication that by this time space for burials was becoming a problem. By 1916, surveyors were asked to advise on whether the area down the hill from the John Cole monument on the main carriageway could be brought into use. A plan for an additional set of catacombs was drawn up, but they do not appear to have been built, although the gullies on the main avenue were altered in 1917.

Trade continued into the 1930s, when plans for improvement were drawn up to celebrate the cemetery's centenary. Fisher, Son and Sibray submitted planting plans to improve the grounds. Electric lighting was installed in the lodges at the end of 1935, and also in the new workshop. However, there had been an even sharper decline in the quality of monument design after the First World War, a national trend also seen within other cemeteries throughout the country. Dubious design decisions were made. The most significant of these was ironically taken in the cemetery's centenary year. The proposal was to change the face of the original landscape layout above the catacombs: the vault heights were to be increased to footpath level excavating above the arches, breaking in the arch tops and pulling down the stone walls to the level required to make 36 reinforced concrete vaults. However, just a few months later, before this plan was implemented, there was extensive subsidence due to heavy rains causing serious collapse of some catacombs and the carriage road. The expense this caused was in the Company's words: serious. However, the plan was implemented, along with the restoration work to repair the flood damage.

Despite the creation of new space for burials, few plots were left for sale, and choice of location was limited. Victorian cemeteries had not been designed to be easily looked after. They were constructed when labour was cheap, materials plentiful and the general public, especially the upper and middle classes, were prepared to spend a great deal on funerals. After the Great War all that changed. The grand Victorian style of funeral seemed almost distasteful in the face of such terrible numbers of war dead. A combination of this change in attitude, the shortage of burial spaces, and a gradual acceptance of cremation as a suitable alternative to burial, caused income to fall drastically. People were also living longer as health and sanitation increased, so turnover was decreasing. Another major factor in the cemetery's decline was the steadily growing costs of labour and materials and an increase in need for maintenance on the site. The omens were not good and the General Cemetery Company quickly went into decline.

A further landslide took place the year after the concrete addition to the main path (1937). It cost more than £3,000 to carry out the necessary repairs, and it was economically impossible to reconstruct the destroyed catacombs so they were converted into small vaults. When the Second World War came it added directly to the Company's problems. Damage occurred in 1941 when Sheffield was the target for German bombs. Throughout the war fees for repairs to bomb damage are documented. The last minute of the General Cemetery Company, in 1949, ominously reads "war damages claim still outstanding".

The Wilderness Years

In the 1950s the Cemetery Company was still selling burial plots in perpetuity although very few burials were taking place (an average of about twelve per year) and most were burials in existing family plots.

The Cemetery Company offered to sell the General Cemetery to the City Council, but after an examination of accounts the Corporation decided it was not financially viable, so the offer was declined. The Cemetery by this time was in a very poor state of repair and overrun with rats. Martin Flannery (an MP in the 1960s, a former teacher) taught in Porter Croft School overlooking the cemetery in 1954. He reported that a child was badly bitten by a rat and another was badly injured by a fall in the cemetery. He added It was so dreadfully overrun and so wild, it was not only an eyesore, but the city had a sense of shame about it (The Sheffield Star April 12 1978).

In 1963 Boden Developments Ltd bought the majority of the shares of the Cemetery Company; intending to use the cemetery for a housing development, although they also planned to retain a small area as a memorial garden. This news caused a great deal of local opposition and protests from owners of plots, and it became rapidly clear that development could not be allowed. Boden Developments were informed officially that a planning application for the site would not succeed. The plan was abandoned and the site became even more derelict, dangerous and overgrown and more of a liability.

In 1974 Sheffield City Council made moves to take over the site with a view to considering alternative uses. To do this the cemetery would have to be closed by the grant of an Order in Council (Burial Act 1853). This was complicated by the fact that plots had been sold by a Deed of Grant in perpetuity and could therefore be inherited as such through wills.

In 1976 the City Council took action under Planning Acts powers to secure urgent maintenance works on the Gatehouse . At the same time Evans Ltd (the parent company for Boden Developments) approached the Council and indicated that they would be willing to transfer the General Cemetery to the city free of charge. They indicated that if the Council refused this offer it would be likely that Evans would consider the voluntary liquidation of the Cemetery Company. The

Cemetery had become too much of a liability. As a result, the Council set about gaining an Act of Parliament to provide a much needed green space for the local community. What this meant in reality was the clearing of the Anglican cemetery. To do this the Council first had to hold a Committee of Enquiry, which involved listening to the views of affected people: plot owners, local residents and community groups. At this time there was no 'Friends of the Cemetery' group, but there was opposition which was documented in the Enquiry papers. The sole Conservative MP for Sheffield at the time was the only politician campaigning for the cemetery's status quo and the rights of the families of those buried there.

The City Council agreed to take on the conservation of the older non conformist cemetery while clearing the Anglican side. It proposed a maintenance programme and some enhancements to the older cemetery for recreational purposes. This plan of action culminated in an Act of Parliament in 1977.

A programme of work began. First the memorials in the cemetery were documented so that the information was available to families wishing to do research. This work included transcribing the epitaphs, names and dates of all the gravestones (including the non conformist cemetery) and was carried out as part of a Manpower Services Commission job creation scheme. The information that was gathered is now held in Sheffield's Archives.

Two sets of photographs of the cemetery were taken by a Council photographer at this time. They give a good impression of what the site was like before the clearance of the site, although provide by no means a complete picture. These photographs demonstrate how overcrowded the Anglican part of the cemetery had become. In general the monuments on the Anglican side were more uniform than those on the non conformist side, and certainly the layout had long since reverted from Marnock's romantic scheme to the Burial Board style of compact and straight-lined rows.

The Council undertook some emergency repairs. Gaps in the perimeter walls were made good, and some of the dangerous structures, particularly the catacombs, were made safe. Next came the exhumation of bodies from the Anglican Cemetery. The Council had been obliged to advertise their plan to clear the graves and some relatives requested exhumations and reburial elsewhere. If no requests were forthcoming bodies were left in position. In 1980, in the face of considerable local opposition from relatives and grave owners, the bulldozers moved in

Council images of the Anglican area before the 1978 clearance

and the demolition of 7,800 gravestones went ahead.

The last burial took place as this destruction began, in 1978.

Some gravestones in the Anglican Cemetery were left in place. The gravestones that were removed were either crushed and used as bedding material for paths, cut and used as edging for paths, or simply buried on site. The ones that were left were not necessarily the most spectacular. The plan was rather to leave a representative group of monuments. The landscaping plans for the non conformist cemetery drawn up by the Planning Department were as a result never carried out, although the cemetery did become a designated Conservation Area in 1986.

Historic Value Recognition

It was in this climate of destruction, decay and lack of maintenance that the Friends of the General Cemetery (FOGC) was established in 1989. The group was set up by a number of concerned residents on Cemetery Road, and followed a well attended public meeting. The aims of the group were to raise awareness about the value of the site, to encourage its use for educational purposes, to protect and ultimately to restore and regenerate the site. FOGC became a registered charity in 1990. The group is a community-based organization with strong local membership.

FOGC immediately began to research the history of the site. Despite the lack of readily available information, the Friends began to conduct tours of the site, and have done every month from 1989. The numbers attending these tours have gradually grown as has the Friends' knowledge and understanding of the site. Tours are now regularly conducted for groups with special interests in geology, flora and fauna, the environment and local history. The universities, Sheffield College and local schools all use the Cemetery as a resource, and call on the Friends for help, advice and information, for talks and tours.

Shortly after FOGC was formed a local businessman took out a lease on the Anglican chapel and submitted a planning application for its conversion into offices. Despite objections from FOGC and others approval was given. This allowed car parking within the cemetery and the creation of a new access into the site. Fortunately the development never took place, and permission for this project has lapsed although the chapel remains in the hands of the developer.

In the meantime FOGC itself took leases on the non conformist chapel and the gatehouse, to protect them from inappropriate development and eventually restore them. In 2002, FOGC were able to begin this work with a project to restore the gatehouse, provide accommodation for a warden and an office for the Friends.

In 1992 the Council undertook some maintenance on the site. A health and safety review led to the removal of some of the historic landscape elements of the cemetery, including the destruction of the retaining wall behind the non conformist chapel. Large areas of the cemetery were fenced off with wooden paling to protect the public from danger and to protect the Council from possible claims. This paling has remained despite being breached in many places. There is considerable public feeling that the fencing is inappropriate, both visually and because it does not allow access to parts of the site people wish to visit.

In the mid 1990s FOGC received several grants for restoration work as well as donations from various sources. This enabled the restoration of the surviving Egyptian gate, Mark Firth's memorial railings, and maintenance work on footpaths and planting. FOGC now has a regular arrangement with Sheffield Conservation Volunteers, BTCV and other groups. Despite this positive work, a spate of serious thefts took place in 1998, and features from many of the historic monuments were stolen. There has also been a great deal of vandalism over the last few years. Buildings and monuments have been defaced and damaged. FOGC now have an office and two full time workers, who work with volunteers on the site and encourage positive use of the cemetery. FOGC also have funding for education development work, using the site as its starting point.

FOGC began negotiating with the Council in the early 1990's to raise the cemetery's profile on the Council's agenda. With the advent of a new chief executive, the Council began to work positively with the Friends and supported our bid for Heritage Lottery Funds to fund the gatehouse restoration. Since then FOGC have established

Bennet s memorial in near the Nonconformist Chapel

a partnership management agreement on the site with Bereavement Services, Sheffield City Council.

The site gained national recognition in 1998 through its inclusion in the National Register of Parks and Gardens of Historic Interest (Grade II). This followed Chris Brooks' report to English Heritage in 1994 in which he cited the cemetery as of national significance and a report on Sheffield's parks by landscape historian Joan Sewell, commissioned by Sheffield Council. The listings of buildings and monuments were increased and upgraded in 1998. In 2000 the section of the Porter Brook at the base of the cemetery also became a designated Conservation Area.

Monument Guide

The following pages provide an introduction to a few of the monuments and the 87,000 people buried in the general Cemetery.

These have not been selected entirely at random, but because these are monuments to people of some interest, and also because their graves are accessible.

George Bassett

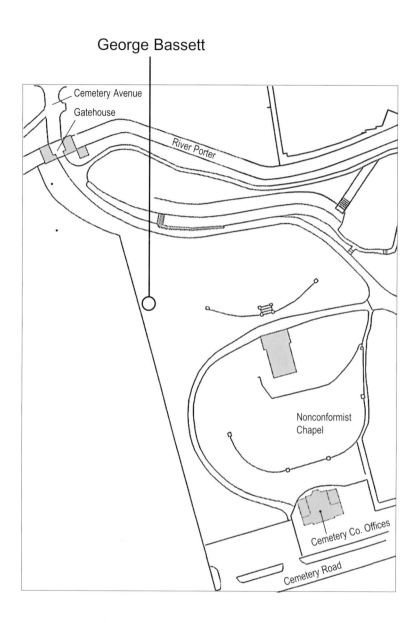

George Bassett

George Bassett of Liquorice Allsorts fame died in 1886 and was buried in the General Cemetery. He started his first sweet shop in the 1840s in Sheffield, gradually increased the number of shops and expanded his business into manufacturing. He was a well known local figure and Lord Mayor in 1876. It was after the death of George Bassett that Liquorice Allsorts were invented. A salesman, presenting a tray of sweets to a shop owner, tripped, and the tray of sweets fell to the floor, all mixed up. The shop owner snapped up an order of 'all sorts' and the brand was born. His memorial is an unimpressive rectangular block with a shield relief on the front, close to the cemetery wall, to the right of the Egyptian archway as you go up the hill.

William Parker

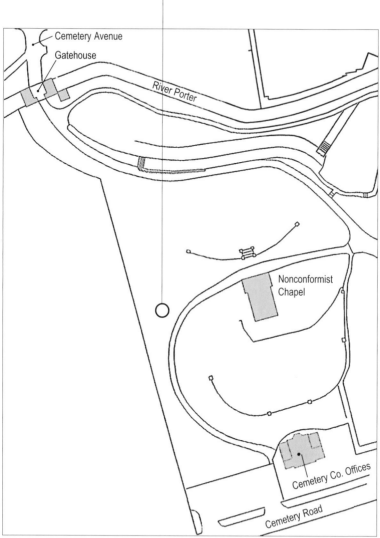

Cemetery Avenue

Gatehouse

River Porter

Nonconformist
Chapel

Cemetery Co. Offices

Cemetery Road

William Parker

An exporter of cutlery and prominent non conformist, Parker died aged 53. This monument was erected in 1837 (Grade II) in esteem by his friends, the 'principal merchants' of the city. This elaborate monument, evoking a monumental design from classical antiquity, was a significant addition in the early cemetery landscape and appears in the first engravings of the cemetery. It is situated to the west of the non conformist chapel. William Parker was a highly respected 'much lamented gentleman', and 1500 people are estimated to have attended his funeral. A few years after his death his wife committed suicide and is buried next to him.

Thomas Burch

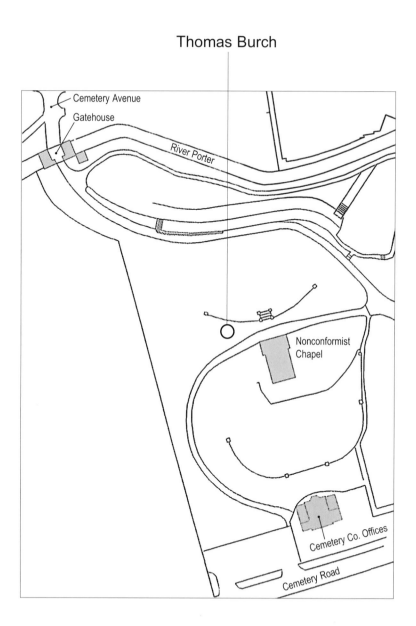

Cemetery Avenue

Gatehouse

River Porter

Nonconformist
Chapel

Cemetery Co. Offices

Cemetery Road

Thomas Burch

In 1870 plans for Alderman Burch's monument were approved. This imposing monument sits in a prime position in front of the non conformist chapel, erected by his widow. The monument is a tall (15 foot) column, on a plinth, topped by an urn, with an enclosure of elaborate wrought iron. An alderman for Sheffield for nearly twenty years he was described in his obituary as a man of *'plodding industry, great natural shrewdness and an unquestionable aptitude for business, which raised him years ago to a good social position.'* His family were clearly intent that this position should be reflected in his memorial.

John Fowler

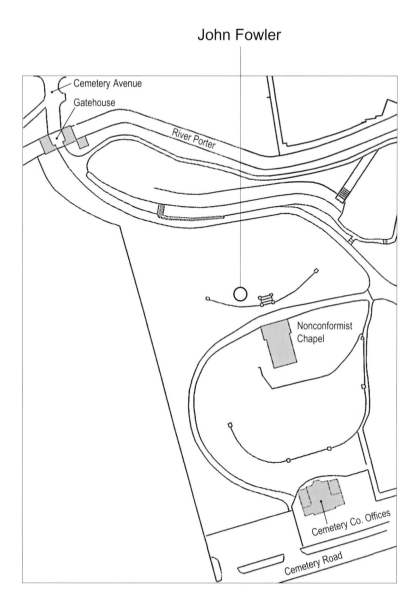

John Fowler

A striking monument erected in 1845 to John Fowler, an engineer. He was the father of the designer of the Forth Bridge, the first underground transport system and Sheffield's impressive Wicker Arch. It is situated just beneath the steps in front of the chapel (to the left as you go down the steps). It was designed and executed by Edwin Smith, whose son contributed the hooded head at the top of the monument (which echoes medieval views about death). It is gated with wrought iron fencing, with a canopied and elaborately arched headstone, supported by columns. The headstone itself has a circular relief sculpture of a broken tree with two acorns on it (possibly symbolising his two sons); and the side pillars engraved with an ivy leaf pattern. Unfortunately, since this photograph was taken, this monument has been badly vandalised.

George Bennet

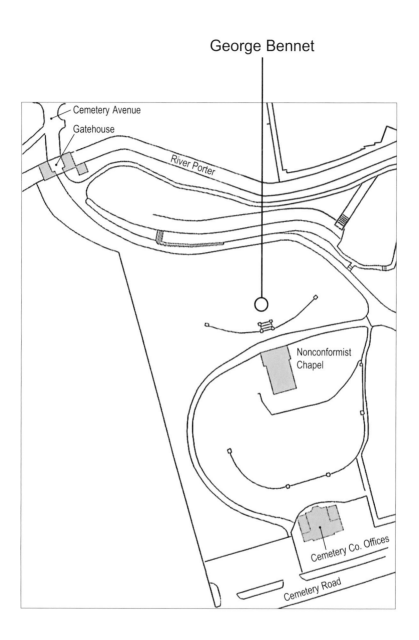

George Bennet

In front of the steps of the non conformist chapel is a monument (Grade II) in memory of George Bennet, a missionary. This is one of the most significantly sited memorials in the cemetery, erected around 1850. Framed by two weeping ash trees, it occupies a key vista from the chapel across the valley. It is 15 feet high and bears a relief sculpture of George Bennet leaning on a globe, with a palm tree behind him, representing his missions across the world. There is a link between this monument and the Montgomery monument placed in front of the Anglican chapel a few years later. The two men were good friends and corresponded over many years and were both campaigners against the slave trade. Bennet went on the longest mission ever undertaken – eight years – and documented his adventures in a journal that now forms the basis of a book.

Original detail from George Bennet s
memorial since vandalised

Margaret Green

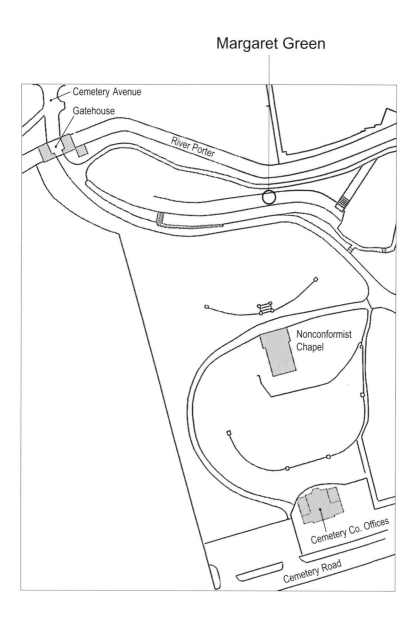

Cemetery Avenue

Gatehouse

River Porter

Nonconformist
Chapel

Cemetery Co. Offices

Cemetery Road

Margaret Green

Margaret's simple memorial lies flat on the catacomb path (three quarters of the way along the path from the gatehouse end) instead of in its original upright position in the Anglican cemetery, moved in 1978. She died in 1869, having surgery for breast cancer, before anaesthetics were introduced. Her gravestone also memorializes ten of her children who died young, and symbolises the plight of women in the nineteenth century - constantly having children, and then suffering an early death. Her gravestone has been the object of research, highlighting the appalling living conditions of city dwellers at that time: Margaret and her family lived close to an abattoir and a refuse tip, and her children all died of diseases associated with poor living conditions such as typhoid and dysentery.

Margaret Green s head stone as it is now (left), and as it was when standing (below).

Cole Brothers

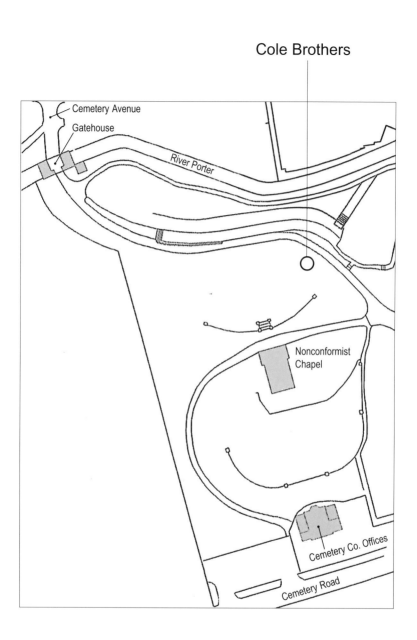

Cemetery Avenue

Gatehouse

River Porter

Nonconformist
Chapel

Cemetery Co. Offices

Cemetery Road

The Cole Brothers

A more dominant memorial to the Cole brothers (John, Thomas and Skelton) than even the large dark obelisk to the right of the main path in the cemetery walking up the hill, is the store named after them in the city centre, which they first established on Fargate in 1847. By 1892 it had grown to four floors employing 350 employees. The brothers all died at the turn of the century (between 1896 and 1902) after life-long service to commerce, the Methodist Society and support to the Jessop Hospital for Women and Totley Orphanage. After their deaths, the Cole family sold their interest to Selfridges who eventually sold the store on to the John Lewis partnership. It moved to its present location in 1963.

Mark Firth

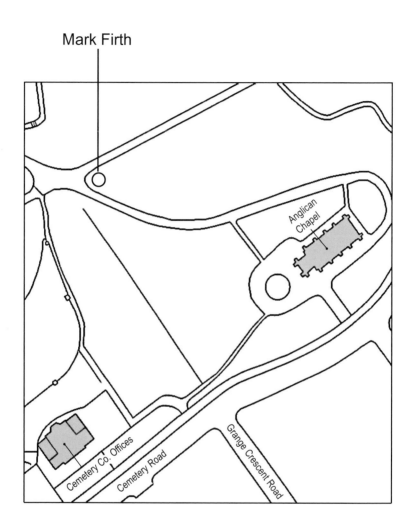

Mark Firth

The Mark Firth memorial (Grade II), was constructed between 1869 and 1876. It stands at the central junction in between the old non conformist and the more recent Anglican cemetery. Made of Aberdeen granite, it was built over a vault topped by a draped urn, and stands about ten feet tall. The monument is in an enclosure with railings made in Firth's own Norfolk works. These substantial railings have elaborate medallion designs.

There is a large slab in front of the monument covering an entrance to the vault. Mark Firth commissioned the monument and chose the spot for the grave, prepared for the loss of one of his daughters.

Mark Firth is one of Sheffield's most famous Victorian figures. He was a highly successful industrialist, establishing the largest steel company in Sheffield, as well as a substantial philanthropist, Lord Mayor and Master Cutler of the city. The grandeur of his funeral ensured it was a well-documented event, and gives an insight into the ritual of the Victorian funeral.

James Nicholson

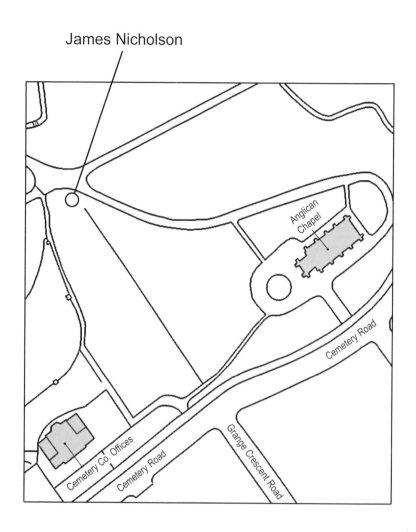

James Nicholson

The James Nicholson memorial, one of the most beautiful in the cemetery, dates from around 1872 (Grade II). It has a principal position on the main path at the central junction. It is a tall chest tomb within a triangular enclosure with a statue of a woman kneeling in prayer on top. It used to have statues of angels on each corner, but these are now gone. The monument commemorates members of the Nicholson family, including Harriet Nicholson who died in 1876. Her husband, who commissioned this monument, died in 1909, and their children are also buried there. The Nicholson family were prominent steel industrialists in Sheffield in the late nineteenth century.

James Montgomery

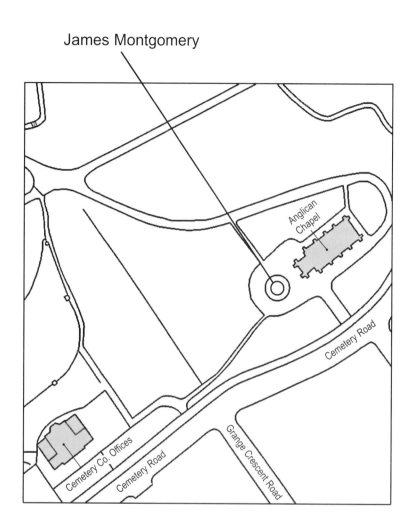

James Montgomery

In 1854 James Montgomery, poet, writer, philanthropist, campaigner, hymn writer, editor of the Sheffield Iris, (which later became the Sheffield Telegraph) died, age 83, and was buried in a wrought iron circular enclosure in front of the Anglican chapel where a monument was erected by public subscription in 1868. Unfortunately the imposing bronze statue of James Montgomery commissioned as his memorial was moved in the upheaval in the cemetery in the 1970s and now sits outside Sheffield cathedral, where his remains were re-interred. A great friend of George Bennet, also buried in the cemetery, they jointly established the Sheffield Sunday School Union. James Montgomery was well known in Sheffield for publishing despite the consequences and was twice sent to jail for his actions. James Montgomery's life and works are well documented, and further information about him is available through Sheffield's library services.

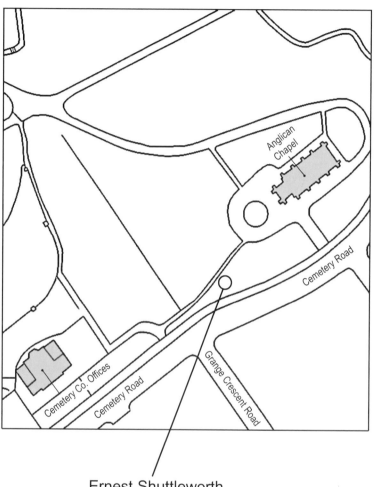

Anglican Chapel

Cemetery Road

Cemetery Co. Offices

Cemetery Road

Grange Crescent Road

Ernest Shuttleworth

Ernest Shuttleworth

This grave memorializes a soldier who died on the first day of the Battle of the Somme (1st July 1916), the most disastrous day in British military history. Over fifty thousand soldiers were killed in the first hour of a futile attack on the German lines. One of these was Ernest Ronald Shuttleworth, who was a Second Lieutenant. This pink granite chest tomb is on the right of the path from the Egyptian gate down to the Anglican chapel. There are many other war graves in the cemetery, from a man who fought at Waterloo, Crimean soldiers through to civilian victims of the Sheffield Blitz.

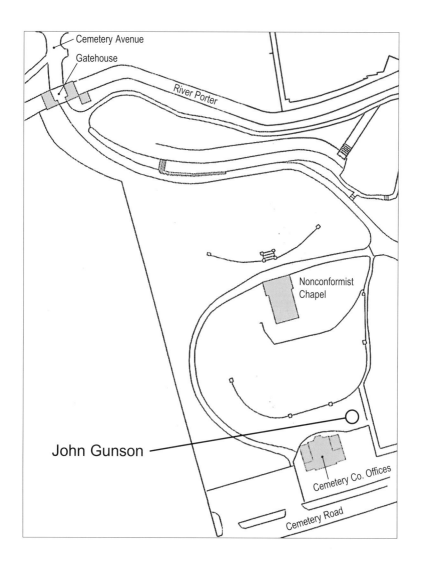

Cemetery Avenue

Gatehouse

River Porter

Nonconformist
Chapel

John Gunson

Cemetery Co. Offices

Cemetery Road

John Gunson

John Gunson's place in Sheffield's history was assured as a result of the devastating flood that engulfed villages above Sheffield and parts of Sheffield in March 1864, when the new Dale Dyke dam burst, unleashing tons of water *'with the noise of thunder, the swiftness of lightening and the force of Niagara'* (Hunter's Hallamshire) onto a sleeping population, killing 240. John Gunson had been involved in overseeing the dam's development and was the assistant engineer responsible for checking the dam, which he did on the day of the disaster. 77 of the flood's victims are buried in the General Cemetery, as well as the man who documented the event, Samuel Harrison. John Gunson was haunted by the disaster, having endured accusations of blame from a furious coroner at the inquest. He died in 1886. A further committee of enquiry exonerated him after his death. His damaged chest tomb is tucked away on a side path near the cemetery offices.

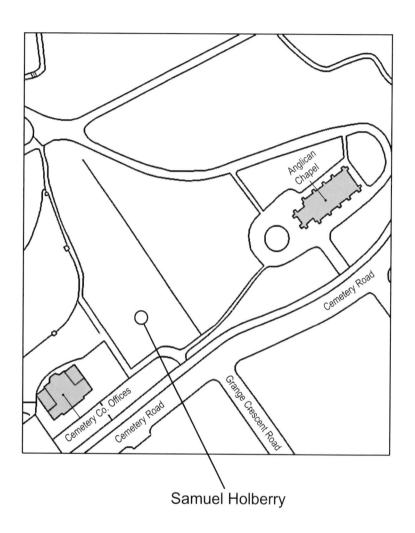

Samuel Holberry

Samuel Holberry

One of the most important memorials in the cemetery is in memory of Samuel Holberry who died in 1842 in York Castle. He was a leading figure in the Chartist movement and was arrested for plotting to seize the Town Hall and a Coaching Inn, which among other actions were carried out for *'advocating what to him appeared to be the true interest of the people of England'* (this is engraved on his stone). All points bar one of the Peoples' Charter that the Chartists advocated have now become law. He died after being placed, illegally, on the treadmill at York prison, aged 27. While in prison he corresponded with several people and these letters were published, and provide a vivid evocation of prison conditions. Following his death he became a martyr symbol and some 50,000 people attended his funeral, an event well documented in the press of the time. His modest headstone lies in a line with his compatriots in arms and wife around him. It is on a clearly marked path through a line of graves in front of the cemetery office.

Postscript

If Worth, Flockton, Marnock, and ultimately Loudon's vision for the General Cemetery had been fulfilled and maintained, it would now be a great planned landscape, its monuments an expression of wealth, piety, power and art, and its planting fully mature. It would also be a central feature of a designed classical landscape along the Porter Valley. However, the 20th century brought dramatic changes in population, town planning and in attitudes to institutional religion. The cemetery can no longer have the importance that was once invested in it. The Porter Valley has developed in a largely unplanned way, the views across the valley obscured by blocks of flats and tree growth.

The cemetery is now a place of two distinct halves - a park which is used by the public for recreational purposes, and an historic site whose monuments, landscape design, and buildings represent something quite different from its original intentions: a relic of an age gone by, a rich resource for reading the past, and a tumbledown romantic haven. We hope its future is secure for future generations.

Bibliography

Friends of the General Cemetery Summary of the Minutes of the General Cemetery Company published by FOGC in 1989.

Mortal Remains, Chris Brooks, pub. Wheaton 1989.

Churchyards of England and Wales, Brian Bailey, Magna Books, 1987.

On the Laying Out of Cemeteries, J C Loudon, Ivelet Books, 1981.

The Art of Death, Nigel Llewelyn, V&A, 1992.

Death in England, Manchester University Press, 1999.